Wheels and Axles

by Anne Welsbacher

Consultant:
Philip W. Hammer, Ph.D.
Assistant Manager of Education
American Institute of Physics

Bridgestone Books
an imprint of Capstone Press
Mankato, Minnesota

Bridgestone Books are published by Capstone Press
151 Good Counsel Drive, P.O. Box 669, Mankato, Minnesota 56002
http://www.capstone-press.com

Library of Congress Cataloging-in-Publication Data
Welsbacher, Anne, 1955–
    Wheels and axles/by Anne Welsbacher.
    p. cm.—(The Bridgestone Science Library)
    Includes bibliographical references and index.
    Summary: Uses everyday examples to show how wheels and axles are simple
machines that make carrying, pushing, and mixing easier.
    ISBN 0-7368-0615-6
    1. Wheels—Juvenile literature. 2. Axles—Juvenile literature. [1. Wheels. 2. Axles.]
I. Title. II. Series.
TJ181.5.W45 2001
621.8'11—dc21

00-025615

Editorial Credits
Rebecca Glaser, editor; Linda Clavel, cover designer; Kia Bielke, illustrator; Katy Kudela,
    photo researcher

Photo Credits
David F. Clobes, cover, 8
Jack Glisson, 12
Kate Boykin, 16
Kimberly Danger, 14, 18
Unicorn Stock Photos/Joseph L. Fontenot, 4; Chris Boylan, 10
Visuals Unlimited/Bill Beatty, 20

1 2 3 4 5 6 06 05 04 03 02 01

Table of Contents

Simple Machines

Wheels and axles are simple machines. Simple machines make work easier or faster. Work is using force to move an object across a distance. Carrying, pushing, and mixing are types of work. Wheels and axles make these types of work easier.

force
anything that changes the speed, direction, or motion of an object

5

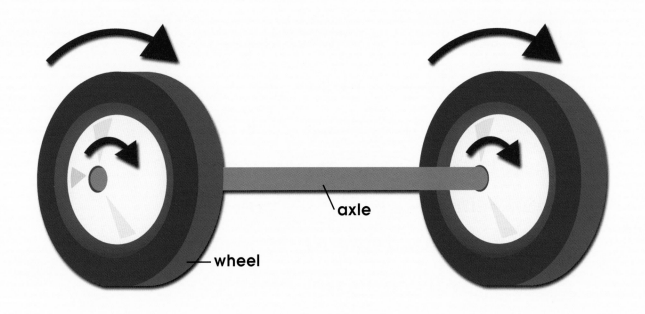

axle

wheel

Parts of a Wheel and Axle

An axle is a rod in the center of a wheel. The wheel turns around the axle. A wheel can spin freely around an axle. A wheel sometimes is fixed to the axle. Axles also can connect two wheels.

More Speed with Wheels and Axles

Wheels and axles help move objects faster. Wheels and axles reduce friction. Rolling something across the ground is easier than sliding it. Pulling your friend in a wagon is easier and faster than carrying him.

friction

a force that slows down objects when they rub against each other

More Force with Wheels and Axles

Wheels and axles can turn a small force into a big movement. A go-cart driver turns the steering wheel to make the go-cart turn. The axle of the steering wheel moves the steering system. This system turns the wheels of the cart.

Cranks

A crank is a handle attached to an axle. A wheel attached to the axle turns when a person turns the crank. A pencil sharpener has a crank. The pedals on a bicycle also work like a crank.

sprockets

sprockets

Sprockets

Sprockets are wheels with teeth.
Bicycles have sprockets. The bicycle
chain fits over the sprockets. The
pedals turn an axle that moves the
front sprocket. The chain moves and
turns the back sprocket. The back
wheel of the bicycle turns.

gears

Gears

Gears are toothed wheels that fit together. An axle moves one gear. The teeth on the gear move another gear. A large gear moving slowly can make a small gear move fast. Gears inside clocks and watches move the hands to show time.

This Way or That Way

Gears can change the direction of force. An egg beater has gears. You turn the crank up and down. The crank turns a gear. This gear turns two other gears. The beaters turn side to side to beat the eggs.

Complex Machines

Simple machines make up complex machines. Wheels and axles are part of rollers. A roller is a large machine that flattens blacktop on streets. An engine turns the axle of a roller.

blacktop
a hard material that covers many streets and parking lots

Hands On: Rolling Pin Roller

A roller is a large machine that flattens blacktop on streets. Rollers use wheels and axles. This activity will show you how wheels and axles make it easier to cover streets with blacktop.

What You Need

Play dough
Table
Rolling pin

What You Do

1. Roll the play dough into a ball.
2. Place the play dough ball on the table. Flatten it with your hand. Keep the dough about 1 inch (2.5 centimeters) thick. Was it easy or hard to flatten?
3. Now try to flatten the dough more by using the rolling pin. Make it very flat and smooth.

It should be easier to make the dough smooth using the rolling pin. You move the axle a short distance. The outside of the rolling pin moves a large distance. A roller works the same way. An engine turns the axle of a roller.

Words to Know

axle (AK-suhl)—a rod in the center of a wheel around which the wheel turns

complex (kahm-PLEKS)—having many parts

force (FORSS)—anything that changes the speed, direction, or motion of an object

gear (GEER)—a toothed wheel that fits into another toothed wheel; gears can change the direction of a force or can transfer power.

sprocket (SPROK-it)—a wheel with a rim of toothlike points that fit into the holes of a chain

work (WURK)—using force to move an object across a distance

Read More

Armentrout, Patricia. *The Wheel.* Simple Devices. Vero Beach, Fla.: Rourke, 1997.

Hodge, Deborah. *Simple Machines.* Starting with Science. Toronto: Kids Can Press, 1998.

Rush, Caroline. *Wheels and Cogs.* Simple Science. Austin, Texas: Raintree Steck-Vaughn, 1997.

Internet Sites

Inventors Toolbox: Simple Machines
http://www.mos.org/sln/Leonardo/InventorsToolbox.html

School Zone, Simple Machines
http://www.science-tech.nmstc.ca/maindex.cfm?idx=1394& language=english&museum=sat&function=link&pidx=1394

Simple Machines
http://www.fi.edu/qa97/spotlight3/spotlight3.html

Index